The Signature

Many often say 'Dream

come True'!

This book says 'Dream

come Bru'!!!

A sip of coffee to warm

up...

Let us usher in with a fun

filled relaxation to mind...

INDEX

SYNOPSIS

We all have got this great
Occasion of portraying our
Signature in this Planet by
the very Nature
surrounding us…!

Our Nature is itself a one
having Miraculous Birth.
Yes! the Cosmos, that is
simply… Our Universe..!.

We have to use the word
'Our Universe', since there
may probably be Other
Universes, even Infinite
number of them…!

Though there have been
Great Developments in
Science & Technology,
still Scientists could not
confirm this one…!

Whatever be those
certitudes…Not at all
matters…, What is needed
is that, We have to sketch a
Happy Signature in this
Planet before we Leave…!
though the Signature may
be Tiny and Invisible…!!!

<u>Focal point of the book:-</u>

"This Itself Proves that there is a Certain Existence of An Unknown and Indescribable Power that No Human Theory can Predict or Match...! And ...**That Is... GOD...!!!**

Inside...!!!

JUST KEEP GOING

"Our life is moving ahead..."

Whether we get loss or profit, it is moving forward. Likewise, whether with happiness or with sorrow, it is STILL progressing!

But, there is one thing…!!!

Is it like, Life is alone moving ahead…?

No...!!!

Everything is moving! Earth is progressing...!!!

It rotates itself, also revolves around our Star 'The Sun' and this entire Solar system is progressing without a valid purpose why it has to do so...!!!

Simply, It is created in such a way that it has to do

so…until the entire system is depleted of all the Energy which is carrying out these VERY motions!

This applies to Life also…!

Until the End, we have to do things that we are intended to do, better to be in a much Simpler way!!!

This simplicity Only will ensure a prolonged LIFE

and can bring LOTS of

Contentment…

As our very topic says…,

"JUST KEEP GOING…"

and Our Signature will

automatically be there in

the Planet…!!!

These are fine for a normal
Life. But we perceive lots
and lots of '**Child deaths**'
even at a pre-mature
stage…!

**What can be their Life's
meaning…?**

The simplest answer is that
"Those children have
already Completed their
Good Going, in the tiny
Quantum of time they

Lived…!!!" achieving the fulfillment.

PRESENT MOMENT

"There are Moments in Life that we normally Disregard and there are also Moments that we Enjoy…"

We normally forget one thing in both cases,…!

That is…,

Having a Moment, is
itself a Great Gift in the
Nature's flow...!!!

This can be understood,
only when we realize how
many People are Leaving
this World without
sustaining their very basic
Life…! Thereby without
having any further
Moments of Living in this
planet…!

That's why, **making**

Ourselves Ready to take

up the very available New

& Present Moment in our

Life, becomes **Very**

Prime…!!!

We have to take-up each

Moment with a Smiling

face and Confidence…!

clearly understanding its

worth and tackling it with

our own GAME PLAN and

IDEALOGY!

This is very possible by

means of developing Good

Passion.

Initially it may seem that

Moments bend our

Life…! but through our

Positive Passion, we can

Bend the Moments as per

our flow of Mind and

Actions…!!!

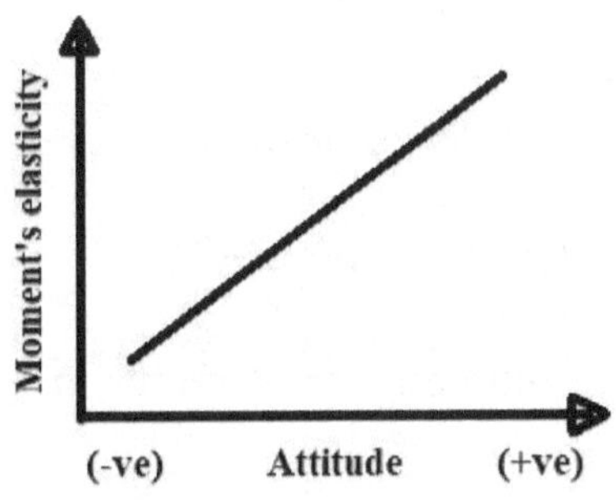

The above Graph shows

this clearly.

Also we can notice…,

whether or not we like it,

the Cosmos/Space

surrounding us will always

be moving infinitely…!

thus Leaving its very

predecessor moments…

towards its successor

moments or positions in

space…, Like,

next position…,

next position…,

next position…

And so on…!!!

Infinitely…!!!

When we apply this nature

of the Cosmos and **Keep**

Moving ahead in Life…

thus "**Enjoying THE**

NOW"…, then surely our

Life will always be

Pleasant…!!!

SOCIETY – A MUCH NEEDED ONE

One thing has become very

VITAL in everybody's

Life…!

Often,

We learn from It…,

We grow with It…,

We care for It…

We even mould It…,

Sometimes We get

moulded by it…!

We plan our most of the

moments keeping an eye

on It…

Yes…!

IT IS THE **SOCIETY**…!!!

Society is the one which is

always surrounding us. We

all have been associated

with it since our very Birth.

'Social interaction' is very essential and more than that, social activities are the key elements to develop prosperity.

Social activities are the driving forces for achieving Meaning to Life…!!!

These activities can be

numerous. !

Such as…, teaching poor

children, nourishing them,

helping orphanages, old

age homes…etc

It will be funny to say…,

On many occasions, a

social activity can be as

simple as a mere visit to a

Tea shop or Bus stand…!

But what is needed out of it

is that, it will be better if

all these small actions…

result in GOOD THINGS

TO SOCIETY!

Truly telling, we should

show our Gratitude in

prayers for living in a

world full of Billions of

people…!

In a **POST APOCALYPTIC**

WORLD, There would be

NO SOCIETY…!, and

Suppose We Survive…,

We have to Look more for

SURVIVAL than for

finding MEANING TO

LIFE…!!!

That situation will

definitely be a Curse…!

Luckily we don't have that

curse at any cost here…!!!

Therefore…,

It will always be nice to

realize… that, We are

Given with a Plenty of

Options… in a Great

Society like this…, to Add

More Meanings… to our

Wonderful life...!!!

THEORIES OF

UNIVERSE

"The Signature that we portray in this World…, in this very Life, is purely a GREAT CHANCE given to Us in this Universe…! "

This very Universe is our
Big Home!

*But where did it come
from…?*

When we analyze this…,

There seems to be Several
Theories for the Universe
especially for its Creation.

‘**Big Bang**’ is the popular
word that comes to our
mind whenever we talk

about the *very Beginning*

of Everything...!

With the Recent

Developments in Spacial

Science and its findings,

accompanied with many

Unanswered Questions,

(***Refer:*** <u>Scientific</u>

<u>Anamoly, Page 38</u>)

Scientists now suggest

that…,

There might have been

Multiple Big Bangs... and

more astonishingly few

other theories suggest that

Big Bangs happen even

now... and at all times…,

resulting in the possibilities

of multiple Universes….

Namely

MULTIVERSES...!!!

Proofs for the above are

beyond the Ability of

Human kind!

One thing we must always

keep in our mind is that

WE ARE BORN TO BE IN

THIS PLANET...! AND

ONLY IN THIS PLANET...!

And it is merely a waste of

time to look for Life on

Other Galaxies based on

the Huge number of Light

Years it takes to start a

possible Civilization in

other Galaxies…! Even to

Reach there…!

[Suppose a **space travel**

takes 1000 years to

reach other Galactic

destination, whether it is

advisable to proceed in that

Space-ship with a plan to

live and have generations

while travelling itself **OR**

to avoid wasting money in

such ideas and

Concentrate on

developing the present

POVERTY In the Society]

It can be well assured that

*the **second Option** is the*

Best...

We are Created here...

and we are intended to

have a purpose and

meaning Only Here in

this very Planet

"EARTH"!!!

And OUR SIGNATURE

also needs to be fine tuned

ONLY HERE…!!!

God's existence proved:

The Best Unanswered

Question in the History of

Mankind can be…

"Whether God exists…?"

People are of many kinds.

One who trusts God, the

other who does Not...

There is one Another type

who partially trust the

existence of God!

Like…,

When they face a problem, they trust God and on other circumstances they don't...!

Scientists always Deny the Existence of God on a majority scale.

Recently they have developed and sent a High Profile Telescope (JW…) to a particular position in Space such that it could capture Images of Light

Rays, even emitted during

the earlier expansion of our

Universe, before Billions

of Years...!

When they observed the

Images taken by this

telescope in the initial

periods (13.8 Billion years

past…), they got

DUMBFOUNDED...!

Scientific Anamoly

explained:

The Image showed FULLY EVOLVED GALAXIES in these INITIAL PERIODS... (*which should not have existed as per the known Science*).

Scientists do not have ANSWERS for this!

They simply replied that the Entire Science has to

be Revised with respect

to this fact...!

Thus it can be very lucid

that **"THERE IS A**

PHENOMENON EXISTING

BEFORE TIME, WHICH IS

ETERNAL, TIMELESS

AND EVERLASTING... An

Unprecedented Power

"GOD"...!!!

Scientists have to look into

this…!!!

MOVE WITH POSITIVITY & HAPPINESS

"Optimistic people achieve the true happiness, whereas being pessimistic can only bring interim happiness…"

All are pro tern ones…!

Won't last long…!

We can see optimism in the society, randomly scattered mostly around **simple things** throughout the world.

Recently I came across one incident which pointed out clearly the importance of positivity and happiness!

It was in front of a cinema theatre around 11.45 am on a Sunny day…

I was just walking from my

home on a holiday to buy

some groceries from our

usual shop.

That cinema theatre was on

the way. Morning show

was in progress. My mind

had prepared myself that

for the AN i.e, the matinee

show, people might come

to that theatre only after

1pm...

My eyes wandered around

that cinema theatre front

gate, the portico and onto

the ticket counter...

No body was there...!!!

Again I watched deeper...,

A surprise…!!!

I could see one youngster

with his newly married

wife waiting there, for the

next show…

In spite of the very hot

sunlight, that youth was

giving a good company to her. He was pointing out at the shops surrounding the theatre and seemed to be sharing his old experiences ... !

Suddenly by seeing something, that youngster ran towards the front gate of the theatre…!

A blind man struggling to surpass a big stone on his

way, was about to lose

control and fall down...!

This youngster went near

that blind man and quickly

helped him, such that he

could go in a safe path!!!

Then he came back to his

girl.

He seemed to continue

telling her about the former

movies he saw in that

theatre...!

Both of them looked like,

they were from a **poor**

economic background.

But their eyes showed

great hopes for a happy

life ahead with what God

has given to them…!

It can be clear that money

is not the only deciding

factor, for having

Happiness in Life.

Through hard work,

simplicity and Positivity,

anyone can achieve

Happiness beyond

doubt…!!!

POOR MAN'S FOOD

"The Signature that we depict in this Life depends also on how Long we live in this Planet"

Food habit can be a parameter of Substantial importance in this regard.

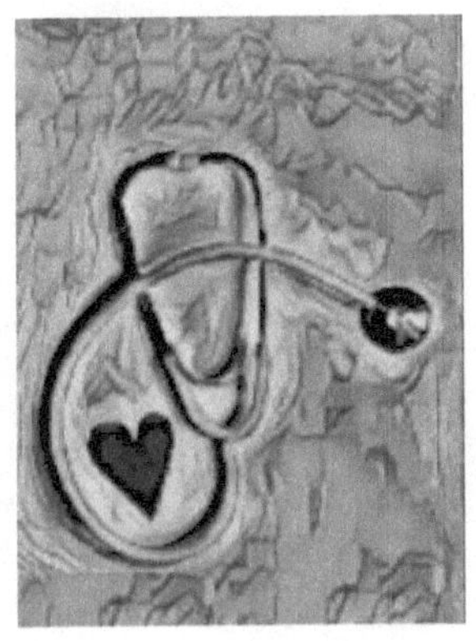

As we all know, there are

two main varieties of

foods, one being 'Veg' and

the other 'Non-veg'.

Irrespective of these two

types, the One particular

item of food to be

considered for Rejection is

THE OILY FOOD and the

DEEP FRIED FOOD.

In both Veg and Non-veg

categories, we have this

particular segment which is

to be Omitted.

This otherwise buildup

unwanted bad cholesterol

level in the Heart which

may lead to Strokes.

There are naturally
available good and
promising foods like **nuts,
cereals, beans, fruits** etc
for good health.

Whatever be the good food
we choose, **people need a
routine physical exercise** for
good digestion and health
maintenance of the human
body.

Physical exercise can be of many types. It can be walking, cycling, jogging on a regular basis.

Even though the time spent on these physical exercises is a little part of the day, it will eventually have a Good impact in the long run.

When we analyze the history of people who lived

long, it will be surprising

to note that, 'POOR MAN'S

FOOD PROMISES

BETTER THAN A RICH

MAN'S FOOD' for

prolonged good Living.

In Tanjore, Tamilnadu,

India, an 113 years old

man is successfully living

on his own earnings with

sound health. (**Courtesy:**

The Indian Express, 20th

Jan 2020).

He is Mohammed Abusali,

popularly known as **'Mittai

Thatha'**. Originally from

Myanmar.

Abusali lives in a rented tenement smaller than 10×10 ft in Aadakaratheru, in Tanjore district of Tamil Nadu.

<u>Highlight of his Interview:</u> When asked about his food habits, He replied to the Interviewer…,

"Often I face poverty…

**And during those times of
economic crisis…, I
simply could afford to eat
a bun and tea from
nearby tea shop…"**

How blessed his simplicity
is…!!!

FACING THE FATE

Many believers tell

"Anything about to happen

is a fate..."

We are all people

belonging to either

Believers or Non believers.

Believers only trust the

concept of Fate.

But when we think deeper,

the word 'Fate' must be

applicable to both the categories of people.

Here is how, it can be…!

For believers, the word fate means '**Happenings as per God's willingness or Almighty's directions'**. This we all knew…

For non believers…, the word fate must literally mean the '**Passage of timely happenings as per**

Universal expansion and

not any super power'.

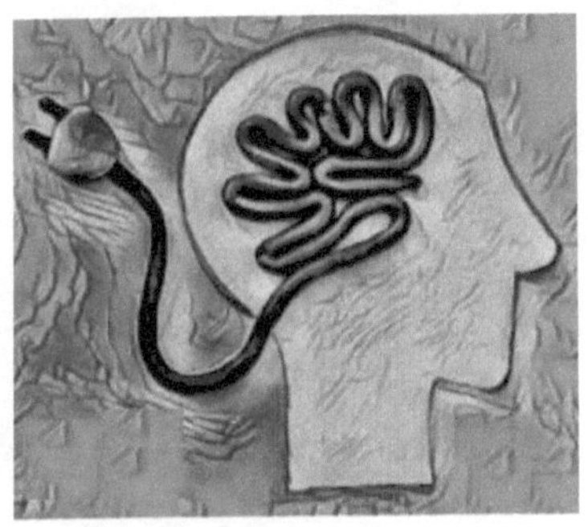

Whatever happened in past

cannot be changed. But

whatever is going to

happen that is things which

are '**yet to become past**'

can be fine tuned.

This needs good passion

and courage for shaping

the future.

This is not practically easy.

There are situations and

work culture in our

everyday life that shows us

less power of control.

When we have good

attitude and passions in life,

we could achieve more

things, thereby it is always

possible to have more

control over our Life in the

flow of time.

This **does not mean** that

we have to be a Magnus

Carlson in Chess or Roger

Federer in Tennis or a

Brian Lara in Cricket.

IN OUR OWN BUSINESS

ITSELF, WE CAN BE THE

HERO...!, once we develop

ourselves to have the full

control in our hands...!!!

For this, the ideology of

'**Postponement of**

sudden decisions in

abominable situations'

can be very much useful.

Life involves some times

many such abominable

situations which are

hateful, dangerous and

avoidable. We must slow

down our pace in making

decisions and immediate

reactions and thereby

achieve good control over

things…!!!

EPILOGUE

WHAT IS NEEDED ?

"Simplicity in doing Right things…"

…is what is needed always!

This book is Not a Religious one… but it is better to refer to a Quote of a Great Being under whose name the entire Human history has been Sundered

into AD and BC…!

Yes…!

Its '**Jesus**'…

He once told…

**"ANYONE WHO HAS TWO
SHIRTS SHOULD SHARE
WITH THE ONE WHO HAS
NONE…!"**

Such phrase of Simplicity

should not only remain in

words but also should be in

Everybody's Actions…!

This can only give Us the

Potential to delineate our

SIGNATURE in this

Planet in this very

Wonderful Life !!!

READER'S PAGE

Dear readers,

My last book was a fiction

story. This time, I just

shared my recent

experiences in this small

book…!

Thanks for reading

Wish you all…,

"Happy days ahead…"

The Signature